This book belongs to

So this is my story

this is my photo

this is my photo

Before I joined my family

ultrasound photo

pregnancy photo

The first person to get the good news about me

my family before I arrived

my baby shower photo

here's another cute photo

And.. Here I am!

my first photo ever

My name is:

I was born on:

The time was:

I was born at:

My length:

My Weight:

another photo of

my very first days

My Birth Announcement

this is my birth announcement

My hospital bracelet

Fun facts
On the day I was born

World leaders:

Famous celebrities:

Popular music:

At the movies:

Succesful TV shows:

Bestselling books:

A loaf of bread costs:

The cost of fuel:

A movie ticket costs:

photo

You were so excited about me, so...

Here's a letter from you to me.
I'm going to love it when I am older.

My prints are super tiny

Hands

my handprint

Feet

my footprint

My first day at home

My home address:

my photo at home   my photo at home

I am 1 month old

photo

photo

When I was one month old:

I could:

Look at me!

photo

photo

photo

I am 2 months old

When I was two months old:

photo

photo

I could:

photo

photo

photo

I am 3 months old

photo

photo

Look at me!

photo

photo

photo

I am 4 months old

When I was four months old:

photo

photo

I could:

Look at me!

photo

photo

photo

I am 5 months old

photo

photo

When I was five months old:

I could:

photo

photo

photo

I am 6 months old

When I was six months old:

photo

photo

I could:

Look at me!

photo

photo

photo

I am 7 months old

When I was seven months old:

photo

photo

I could:

photo

photo

photo

I am 8 months old

When I was eight months old:

photo

photo

I could:

photo

photo

photo

I am 9 months old

When I was nine months old:

photo

photo

I could:

Look at me!

photo

photo

photo

I am 10 months old

When I was ten months old:

I could:

photo

photo

I could:

photo

photo

photo

I am 11 months old

I could:

photo

photo

photo

photo

photo

I am 12 months old

When I was twelve months old:

photo

photo

I could:

photo

photo

photo

My first scribble

Some of my favorite things during my first year

The book I loved most _______________________________

The song I couldn't stop listening to _______________________________

What always made me laugh _______________________________

I loved to eat _______________________________

My favorite toy _______________________________

My best friend _______________________________

Here I am with my favorite:

photo

photo

Here I am with my favorite:

I am 1 year old! 

photo of my birthday

photo of my birthday

I celebrated with ____

Something special to remember

photo of my birthday

 # I am 2 years old! 

photo of my birthday

photo of my birthday

photo of my birthday

I am 3 years old!

photo of my birthday

photo of my birthday

I celebrated with

Something special to remember

photo of my birthday

# I am 4 years old! 

photo of my birthday

photo of my birthday

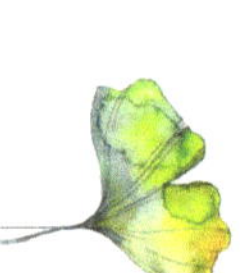

I celebrated with ____

Something special to remember

photo of my birthday

I am 5 years old!

photo of my birthday

photo of my birthday

I celebrated with

Something special to remember

photo of my birthday

My first day at school

photo at school   photo at school

My teacher:

My school name:

MY FAMILY TREE

I am growing

Date	Age	Weight	Height

My teeth development

Date when appeared	My tooth	Date when lost
	1st	
	2nd	
	3rd	
	4th	
	5th	
	6th	
	7th	
	8th	
	9th	
	10th	
	11th	
	12th	
	13th	
	14th	
	15th	
	16th	
	17th	
	18th	
	19th	
	20th